ISBN 978-0-259-10272-4
PIBN 10548740

1 MONTH OF
FREE
READING

at
www.ForgottenBooks.com

By purchasing this book you are eligible for one month membership to ForgottenBooks.com, giving you unlimited access to our entire collection of over 700,000 titles via our web site and mobile apps.

To claim your free month visit:
www.forgottenbooks.com/free548740

English
Français
Deutsche
Italiano
Español
Português

www.forgottenbooks.com

Mythology Photography **Fiction**
Fishing Christianity **Art** Cooking
Essays Buddhism Freemasonry
Medicine **Biology** Music **Ancient
Egypt** Evolution Carpentry Physics
Dance Geology **Mathematics** Fitness
Shakespeare **Folklore** Yoga Marketing
Confidence Immortality Biographies
Poetry **Psychology** Witchcraft
Electronics Chemistry History **Law**
Accounting **Philosophy** Anthropology
Alchemy Drama Quantum Mechanics
Atheism Sexual Health **Ancient History**
Entrepreneurship Languages Sport
Paleontology Needlework Islam
Metaphysics Investment Archaeology
Parenting Statistics Criminology
Motivational

United States Department of the Interior, Douglas McKay, Secretary

Fish and Wildlife Service, John L. Farley, Director

CREEL CENSUS AND EXPENDITURE STUDIES,

MISSOURI RIVER BASIN

Compiled by

A. J. Nicholson, Fish and Wildlife Administrator

and

H. Milton Borges, Fishery Research Biologist

Special Scientific Report: Fisheries No. 141

Washington, D. C.

March, 1955

CONTENTS

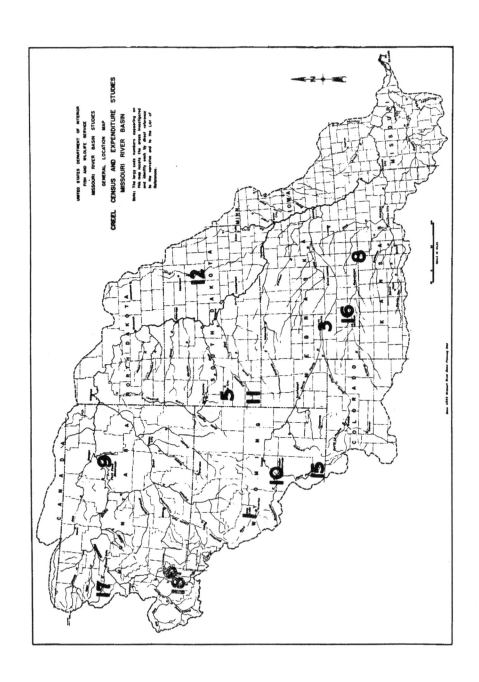

UNITED STATES DEPARTMENT OF INTERIOR
FISH AND WILDLIFE SERVICE
MISSOURI RIVER BASIN STUDIES
GENERAL LOCATION MAP
CREEL CENSUS AND EXPENDITURE STUDIES
MISSOURI RIVER BASIN

CREEL CENSUS AND EXPENDITURE STUDIES
MISSOURI RIVER BASIN, 1947-52

The Office of Missouri River Basin Studies, Fish and Wildlife Service,
conducted 13 creel-census and fisherman-expenditure studies under a variety of
conditions in the Missouri River Basin during the period 1947 through 1952.
Since several of the studies covered more than one body of water, information
is available on a total of 26 areas: 7 warm-water reservoirs or lakes, 3 warm-
water streams, 11 cold-water reservoirs or lakes, and 5 cold-water streams.

This paper summarizes data on fisherman use, yield to the fisherman,
and fisherman's expenditures for these 26 areas. Methods used in the studies
are briefly described. Principal characteristics are given for each area, together with information on type and period of coverage, period of estimates,
and manner of handling expenditure data.

METHODS

Except for minor refinements made during the course of the studies,
and limitation on coverage of certain areas, similar methods were used for all
studies; and it is believed that results are generally comparable.

Studies were usually started on the opening of the fishing season in
the spring and continued throughout the summer. In some cases, limited observations and fisherman contacts were made in the fall (and winter, if fishing
was permitted then) in order that an estimation could be made of pressure and
yield for the entire season. Data were obtained by checking stations or by
patrol, checking stations being used whenever possible. Large reservoirs (or
lakes) and extensive sections of streams were divided into check areas which
were covered on alternate days or alternate mornings and afternoons. Coverage

was made on all Saturdays, Sundays, and holidays. Effort was made to contact as many fishermen as possible. Parties seen but not contacted were recorded daily. In some instances estimates were made of the number of uncontacted or unseen parties.

Data obtained from fishermen relative to use and yield of the fishery included the number of fishermen in each party, home address, type of fishing (boat or shore), time spent fishing, and number and species of fish caught. Data ordinarily were secured from one member of the party. All the fishermen in one boat or all the occupants of one or more automobiles who fished together were treated as a party.

Creel data usually were compiled for 2-week periods (1-week periods were used in a few instances) and applied to fishermen observed but not contacted and those estimated to be present in the same period of time. Estimates of total use and yield for each check area were based on summation of estimates for the 2-week periods.

A few studies--those on Cottonwood Lake, Angostura Reservoir, Harry Strunk Lake, and the 5.5-mile reach of the North Platte River--were limited samplings. These samplings were based on an analysis of several of the intensive creel censuses (19)[1]. This analysis revealed that coverage could be reduced to a check of three days, one each month, providing a Sunday or holiday, a Saturday, and a weekday were represented. It was concluded that the error in estimates resulting from such reduced coverage probably would not increase by more than 15 percent any error that might have existed in the estimates derived from an intensive study.

- -

[1] Parenthetical figures through text and in accompanying tables refer to reference numbers in list of references.

L

2

Fisherman expenditures were divided into four categories; Transportation, Trip, Investment in equipment, and Annual (recurring). All four types of expenditures were secured in the field in the first few studies. In later studies, only transportation and trip expenses were obtained in the field and investment and annual expenses were applied, either from a special survey of Montana fisherman (7) or from data obtained on similar nearby areas. Expenditure data were limited to a sample of 10 percent or less or the total number of fishermen contacted in the earlier studies. In the later studies, trip and transportation expenses were secured from virtually all the fishermen contacted for creel data.

Expenditure data included the point of origin of the trip (for miles traveled); days in the trip; expenditures per day for food, lodging, bait, rentals, guide service, and miscellaneous items such as refreshments, film, and ice. The earlier studies included questions on cost of equipment, days used per year, life expectancy, cost of maintenance, cost of license and days used per year, contributions to conservation causes, and similar expenses. All expenditures were reduced to a fisherman-day basis. A rate of 7 cents per mile was applied to mileage per person per day to derive the daily expenditure per person for transportation.

Expenditure data were compiled on a seasonal basis, either for the study area as a whole or for major segments for which transportation costs were significantly different.

Some of the calculations in the accompanying tables were shown in the original references as rounded figures or were based on rounded figures. For the purpose of this paper, all calculations were remade, using basic unrounded figures, and have been shown in their unrounded form, therefore, there

3

are minor variations in some of the figures, especially for expenditure, from those shown in the original references.

DESCRIPTION OF STUDY AREAS

Warm-water reservoirs or lakes

Ocean Lake, Wyoming (1, 2), is in the Riverton Irrigation Project on the plains of the Wind River Basin. It is 6,100 acres in size. It occupies a natural, saucer-shaped, shallow depression and is fed primarily by seepage and return flows from the irrigation project. Water levels fluctuate very little. Aquatic vegetation is abundant.

Access is good and boat-rental facilities are available. About half the fishermen using the lake during the study came from within 50 road-miles of the lake. About 85 percent of the fishermen came from within 200 miles.

In order of abundance in the catch, black crappie, largemouth black bass, bluegill, green sunfish, and burbot were taken.

Type and period of coverage: Intensive checks, June 22 through September 23, 1947, and June 2 through September 12, 1948. Limited checks during both winters.

Period of estimates: Estimates of use and yield for entire year in both 1947 and 1948.

Expenditures for equipment and annual items: Obtained in field.

Other expenditure items: Transportation expenditures derived for both summer periods and one winter period. The one winter-period transportation expenditure applied in both winters. Trip expenditures determined in 1948 for both summer and winter periods and applied to the respective periods in 1947.

Lake Maloney, Nebraska (3, 4), is in the west-central portion of the

State about 7 miles south of the city of North Platte. It is an off-stream regulatory reservoir of 1,670 surface acres, built for storage and regulation of irrigation water and production of power. Maximum depth is about 31 feet. The annual fluctuation did not exceed 5 feet during the 2-year study.

Access to the area is excellent by a direct road from the city of North Platte. Approximately 97 percent of the fishermen contacted were residents of Nebraska, of which 84 percent came from the town of North Platte.

White crappie compised about 95 percent of the take. Carp, yellow pikeperch, channel catfish, suckers, black bullheads, northern pike, largemouth black bass, and a few trout were among the other species taken.

Type and period of coverage: Intensive checks from April 4 through September 14, 1948, and April 23 through September 4, 1949. Limited checks during the fall and winter.

Periods of estimates: Estimates of use and yield for entire year in both 1948 and 1949.

Expenditures for equipment and annual items: Obtained in the field.

Other expenditure items: Obtained in summer of 1949 only but applied throughout both years.

Fort Peck Reservoir, Montana (9), completed in 1939, is on the Missouri River in northeastern Montana. This 245,000-acre reservoir was built to provide storage of water for navigation, flood control, irrigation, and production of hydroelectric power. The greatest depth is 225 feet. Water levels fluctuated about 20 feet during the period of study. Access to the reservoir is good only in the vicinity of the dam; elsewhere, roads are generally poor or nonexistent. More than 80 percent of the fishermen came from within a 50-mile radius.

Nonresident parties constituted only 3 percent of the total number.

The three principal species in the catch in order of abundance were yellow perch, goldeye, and sauger. These fishes constituted about 90 percent of the catch. Rainbow and brown trout and channel catfish were among the other species taken.

Type and period of coverage: Intensive checks in vicinity of dam, May 4 through September 14, 1948, June 2 through September 14, 1949, and April 15 through September 14, 1950. Limited checks in vicinity of dam, during spring, winter, and fall of 1949 and 1950. Limited checks of outlying portion of reservoir during summer period all three years.

Period of estimates: Estimates of use and yield for entire year, in each year.

Expenditures for equipment and annual items: Obtained in field in 1948 and 1949, applied from special survey of fishermen from adjacent Valley and Roosevelt Counties (7) in 1950.

Other expenditure items: Obtained in summer periods only, but applied throughout respective years.

Split Rock Lakes, Montana (17), are a chain of weedy ponds, totaling about 120 acres, on the Sun River Irrigation Project on the eastern slope of the northern Rocky Mountains. These ponds are fed by seepage water from an irrigation canal. Access to the area is moderately good in dry weather.

Northern pike comprised 96 percent of the catch. Yellow perch and largemouth bass also were taken.

Type and period of coverage: Checked on alternate week basis, May 20 through September 30, 1951.

6

Period of estimates: Estimates of use and yield for above period only
but use through remainder of season (October 1 through November 15) thought to
be negligible.

Expenditures for equipment and annual items: Applied from special
survey of Montana fishermen (7).

Other expenditure items: Single figure derived for all areas below
Gibson Reservoir in North Fork Sun River study and applied to each area.

Angostura Reservoir, South Dakota (11), is a multiple-purpose reservoir on the Cheyenne River on the southeastern slope of the Black Hills. It
is 5,600 acres in size. The dam was completed in 1949, and the reservoir was
opened to fishing on July 1, 1952.

Fluctuation was negligible during the period of study, and the reservoir remained at near maximum capacity. The maximum depth is about 137 feet.

Roads varying from good to poor provide access to most of the shore,
but the various fishing areas are not directly connected and considerable travel
is necessary to go from one area to another. Fifty-five percent of the anglers
came from within a radius of less than 50 road-miles. An additional 27 percent
came from between 51 and 100 miles, mostly from Rapid City, S. Dak., 78 miles
from the reservoir. Approximately 13 percent of the fishermen were nonresidents.

Yellow perch, black bullhead, green sunfish, and rainbow trout in that
order comprised about 97 percent of the catch. Yellow pikeperch, largemouth
bass, crappies, and channel catfish also were recorded.

Type and period of coverage: Periodic checks (19), July 1 through
October 12, 1952.

Period of estimates: Estimates of use and yield for above period only.

Expenditures for equipment and annual items: Applied from other studies (1, 3, 8).

Other expenditure items: Applied to above period.

Cottonwood Lake, South Dakota (12), is an enlarged natural lake in the southeastern part of the State. The lake has a surface area of 1,450 acres and a maximum depth of 10 feet. It is fed from Medicine Creek and local drainage. Fluctuation normally is limited, and aquatic vegetation, principally sago pondweed, is common. Access is excellent, and there are roads around most of the lake.

Fishermen were mainly local residents, most of whom came from within a radius of 50 miles. Nonresidents comprised only 2.5 percent of the total number. Yellow perch, black bullhead, and yellow pikeperch in that order made up 99 percent of the catch. Largemouth bass and green sunfish also were taken.

Type and period of coverage: Periodic checks (19), May 1 through September 21, 1952. Limited checks in fall and winter.

Period of estimates: Estimates of use and yield included in this paper for period May 1 through September 21 only.

Expenditures for equipment and annual items: Applied from other studies (1, 3, 7, 9).

Other expenditure items: Applied to above period.

Harry Strunk Lake, Nebraska (16), is a multiple-purpose reservoir constructed in 1949 on Medicine Creek near the town of Cambridge in the south-central part of Nebraska. The impoundment was opened to fishing on April 1, 1952. It has a surface area of 1,768 acres. Maximum depth of the reservoir is about 64 feet. Fluctuation was negligible during the period of study. The reservoir is approached by county roads from many directions.

8

About 90 percent of the anglers were from Nebraska, but many of these came from cities as far away as Omaha (265 miles). White crappie and black bullhead were the principal species caught; carp, bluegill, largemouth black bass, channel catfish, black crappie, and yellow pikeperch were the other species of importance.

Type and period of coverage: Periodic checks (19), April 1 through September 1, 1952.

Period of estimates: Estimates of use and yield, April 1 through October 20.

Expenditures for equipment and annual items: Applied from other studies (3).

Other expenditure items: Transportation expenditures obtained in field. Trip expenditures applied from other studies (3).

Warm-water streams

Missouri River, Montana (9), below Fort Peck Dam was a study area confined chiefly to tailwater and connecting borrow pit areas. About 12 river-miles were included in the study. Volume of flow is reasonably stable and access to the area is generally good. The water is fairly clear and cold. The fishes in order of abundance in the catch were sauger, goldeye, and yellow perch. Rainbow and brown trout and channel catfish also were recorded.

The fishery served principally local people who came from within a 50-mile radius.

For type and period of coverage, period of estimates, expenditures for equipment and annual items, and other expenditure items, see Fort Peck Reservoir.

Republican River, Nebraska and Kansas (8), was studied on a 43-mile reach from south-central Nebraska into north-central Kansas. The river bed is primarily sand and varies in width from 250 feet to about 675 feet. The flow fluctuates from flood condition to extremely low water.

Access to the river is reasonably good during dry weather. Ninety-five percent of the parties traveled a distance of less than 50 miles. Channel catfish comprised about 76 percent of the catch. Carp, flathead catfish, fresh-water drum, shovelnose sturgeon, black bullhead, and carpsuckers also were taken.

Type and period of coverage: Intensive checks, April 22 through September 15, 1951. Limited checks earlier in the spring and in the fall.

Period of estimates: Estimates of use and yield for entire year.

Expenditures for equipment and annual items: Applied from Lake Maloney study (3).

Other expenditure items: Obtained in summer period and applied throughout the year.

Medicine Creek, Nebraska (16), was studied over a 1-3/4 mile-reach at the tailwater below Harry Strunk Lake dam. Many of the fish taken were spilled into the stream from the reservoir. Largemouth black bass, yellow pikeperch, channel catfish, carp, and bullhead in that order comprised the major portion of the catch. Most of the fishing was done in connection with fishing in Harry Strunk Lake.

Type and period of coverage: General observations of fishing, spring and summer of 1951 and 1952.

Period of estimates: Entire year, 1951 and 1952, but only estimates for 1951 included in this paper.

10

Expenditures for equipment and annual items, and other expenditure items: Applied from Harry Strunk Lake.

Cold-water Reservoirs

Deerfield Reservoir, South Dakota (5, 14), 435 acres in size, is on Castle Creek in the center of the Black Hills. Completed in 1945, the reservoir was constructed to provide storage and regulation of water for irrigation and municipal use. Fluctuations had not exceeded 6 feet prior to the 1950 study. This reservoir is somewhat unusual in that aquatic vegetation occurred in most of the shallow areas.

Access to the area is moderately good during dry weather. Fishermen came largely from within a radius of 50 miles. The species most commonly represented in the creels were, in order of abundance, rainbow trout, white sucker, brown trout, and brook trout. Mountain suckers and green sunfish also were taken.

Type and period of coverage: Intensive checks, May 1 through September 30, 1949 and 1950.

Period of estimates: Estimates of use and yield for above periods--the fishing season.

Expenditures for equipment and annual items: Obtained in field in 1949.

Other expenditure items: Obtained in 1950, combined with equipment and annual expenditures, and applied to both years.

Pathfinder Reservoir, Wyoming (10), was completed in 1909. It is on the North Platte River in the south-central part of Wyoming and provides storage for irrigation and power. The reservoir fluctuated about 43 feet during the period of study. It has a surface area of 22,600 acres.

11

Access to the area is only fair. There are no public recreational developments, and boat launching sites are few. The fishery is mainly of local value. The species taken were rainbow, brown, brook, cutthroat, and hybrid trout; suckers; and carp.

Type and period of coverage: Intensive checks, April 29 through September 16, 1951. Limited checks during winter, spring, and fall.

Period of estimates: Entire year.

Expenditures for equipment and annual items: Applied from special survey of Montana fishermen (7).

Other expenditure items: Obtained in summer period and applied throughout year.

Alcova Reservoir, Wyoming (10), the diversion impoundment of the Kendrick Irrigation Project, is on the North Platte River downstream from Path-finder Reservoir. It was constructed in 1938. Annual fluctuation is extreme, but during the period of study the difference in pool levels was only about 19 feet. It is 2,500 acres in size. The whole northwest shore and three main points on the southeast shore are readily accessible. The fishery is primarily of local interest. The species taken were the same as in Pathfinder Reservoir.

For type and period of coverage, period of estimates, expenditures for equipment and annual items, and other expenditure items, see Pathfinder Reservoir.

Gibson Reservoir, Montana (17), is an irrigation storage reservoir of 1,360 acres on the North Fork Sun River, a cold, clear mountain stream. The reservoir, which has a maximum depth of about 180 feet, is subject to consid-erable fluctuation.

12

Access is poor. Most of the fishermen using the area are residents. Rainbow, cutthroat, and brook trout in that order comprised 99 percent of the catch. Suckers were taken.

Type and period of coverage: Intensive checks, May 20 through September 30, 1951.

Period of estimates: Above period only, but use during remainder of season thought to be negligible.

Expenditures for equipment and annual items: Applied from special survey of Montana fishermen (7).

Other expenditure items: Derived separately for this area.

Diversion Reservoir, Montana (17), is the backwater of a diversion structure of the Sun River Irrigation Project on the North Fork Sun River, 2 miles below Gibson Reservoir. It has a surface area of 100 acres. Water is maintained at a relatively stable level and the area is readily accessible. Most of the fishermen are residents of Montana. Rainbow, brook, and cutthroat trout comprised 99 percent of the take. Suckers and Rocky Mountain whitefish also were recorded.

For type and period of coverage, period of estimates, and expenditures for equipment and annual items, see Gibson Reservoir.

Other expenditure items: See Split Rock Lakes.

Willow Creek Reservoir, Montana (17), is an offstream irrigation reservoir on the plains at the foot of the eastern slope of the northern Rocky Mountains on the Sun River Irrigation Project. Surface area is 1,400 acres. Annual fluctuation is about 15 to 30 feet. Access is moderately good during dry weather. The fishermen were from the immediate area. The catch was primarily suckers, and

13

rainbow, brook, and cutthroat trout.

For type and period of coverage, period of estimates, and expenditures for equipment and annual items, see Gibson Reservoir.

Other expenditure items: See Split Rock Lakes.

Pishkun Reservoir, Montana (17), 1,550 acres in size, is an offstream impoundment of the Sun River Irrigation Project. It is similar to Willow Creek Reservoir with the exception that it remains fairly stable during most of the year. It is reasonably accessible during good weather. Rainbow trout were most frequently caught. Grayling, brook and cutthroat trout, perch, and suckers comprised the remainder of the catch.

For type and period of coverage, period of estimates, and expenditures for equipment and annual items, see Gibson Reservoir.

Other expenditure items: See Split Rock Lakes.

Tunnel Lake, Montana (17), is a former pothole which is fed by seepage from an irrigation canal. It is on the Sun River Irrigation Project. It has a surface acre of 20 acres. It is reasonably accessible during good weather and is fished primarily by local residents. The catch was largely rainbow and brown trout. Cutthroat and brook trout and suckers also were taken.

For type and period of coverage, period of estimates, and expenditures for equipment and annual items, see Gibson Reservoir.

Other expenditure items: See Split Rock Lakes.

Wood Lake, Montana (17), on a tributary of the South Fork of the North Fork Sun River, is a 20-acre, natural mountain lake subject to no fluctuation. It is readily accessible by automobile during dry weather. Although it is fished primarily by local residents, its rather remote location necessitates considerable travel. Cutthroat, brook, and rainbow trout were taken in almost equal numbers.

Type and period of coverage: Intensive checks, June 24 to July 7, 1951.

Period of estimates: Above period only but thought to represent most of the fishing.

Expenditures for equipment and annual items: See Gibson Reservoir.

Other expenditure items: Derived separately for this area.

Madison Reservoir, Montana (18), on the Madison River in the northern Rocky Mountains, was built in 1908 for power production. It is 3,800 acres in size. Aquatic-plant beds are abundant in the upper part of the reservoir. Fluctuation has been as great as 8 feet, but normally is not that pronounced. Access is good on two-thirds of the shoreline.

Most of the fishermen were residents of Montana. Although rainbow and brown trout comprised most of the catch, 11 percent of the take was suckers. Brook and cutthroat trout, Rocky Mountain whitefish, suckers, and grayling also were recorded.

Type and period of coverage: Intensive checks, May 21 through September 30, 1950. Limited checks in fall.

Period of estimates: General fishing season, May 21 through November 15.

Expenditures for equipment and annual items: Applied from special survey of Montana fishermen (7).

Other expenditure items: Single figure derived for this area and the lower section of the Madison River covered in 1950 and applied to both fisheries.

Hebgen Lake, Montana (18), on the upper portion of the Madison River, was built in 1915 for power production. The maximum depth of this 13,400-acre reservoir is 70 feet, and annual drawdown is usually around 10 to 15 feet. Aquatic vegetation is well established in Hebgen Reservoir and bordering marshes.

Access is excellent. A large number of nonresident fishermen use this area, apparently because of its proximity to Yellowstone National Park. Although rainbow and brown trout comprised the major portion of the take, Utah chub frequently were caught and cutthroat trout, Rocky Mountain whitefish, and suckers also were taken.

Type and period of coverage: Semi-intensive checks, May 21 through September 30, 1952.

Period of estimates: Fishing season, same as above period.

Expenditures for equipment and annual items: See Madison Reservoir.

Other expenditure items: Single figure derived for this area and the upper section of the Madison River covered in 1952 and applied to both fisheries.

Cold-water streams

Middle Section, West Gallatin River, Montana (6, 13). The West Gallatin River is located on the east slope of the Rocky Mountains in southwestern Montana. Most of the drainage basin is above 5,000 feet and is covered with coniferous forests. The middle section, 28 miles in length, is subject to extensive diversion of water for irrigation purposes, and the gradient is moderate. Access is excellent. Most fishing in this area was by residents of Bozeman, about 9 miles away.

Rainbow, brook, brown, cutthroat, and hybrid trout, Rocky Mountain whitefish, and suckers were taken in the West Gallatin River.

Type and period of coverage: Intensive checks, May 22 through September 30, 1949, and May 21 through September 30, 1950. Limited checks in fall of both 1949 and 1950.

16

Period of estimates: Fishing season, May 22 through November 15, 1949, and May 21 through November 15, 1950.

Expenditures for equipment and annual items: Obtained in the field in 1949.

Other expenditure items: Obtained in 1950, combined with equipment and annual expenditures obtained in 1949, and applied to both years.

Upper Section, West Gallatin River, Montana (6, 13). The upper section of the West Gallatin is typical of most high Rocky Mountain streams. The gradient is steep to moderate, the average width is approximately 60 feet, and pools and riffles are in close succession in the 55-mile reach studied. Flows are reasonably stable except during annual flood stage.

Access to the upper section is excellent. The percentage of nonresident fishermen was high because of the natural attractiveness of the area and proximity to Yellowstone National Park. The same species of fish were taken in the upper section as in the middle section, but brown trout were less prevalent than in the middle section.

Type and period of coverage: Limited checks, May 22 through September 30, 1949.

Period of estimates: Fishing season, May 22 through September 30, 1949.

Expenditures for equipment and annual items, and other expenditure items, applied from Middle Section, West Gallatin River.

Fremont Canyon, Wyoming (10), comprised a 4-mile stretch of the North Platte River lying between Alcova and Pathfinder Reservoirs. It is difficult of access in its canyon location. Fishermen were mainly residents from within 50 miles. Suckers comprised about 66 percent of the take and rainbow trout

17

comprised about 30 percent. Ca.p, brown trout, and hybrid trout also were taken.

For type and period of coverage, period of estimates, expenditures for equipment and annual items, and other expenditure items, see Pathfinder Reservoir.

Upper Section, North Fork Sun River, Montana (17). The North Fork Sun River lies on the eastern slope of the northern Rocky Mountains. The upper section is composed of two forks, typical mountain streams with an abundance of pools and riffles. Each fork is about 60 feet wide. About 50 miles of river were included in the study. Although this area is accessible only by horseback or on foot, at least seven dude ranchers make a business of packing people into the area. Use of the area was mainly by nonlocal people—78 percent came from over 50 miles away. Rainbow, cutthroat, and brook trout in that order comprised the take.

Type and period of coverage, period of estimates, and expenditures for equipment and annual items, see Gibson Reservoir.

Other expenditure items: Derived separately for this area.

Middle Section, North Fork Sun River, Montana (17). The Middle Section is between Gibson Dam and Diversion Reservoir. It is about 80 feet wide and 3 miles long. Here the river flows through a narrow canyon and is characterized by large, deep pools and turbulent riffles. Access is good from a road which parallels the stream. Fishermen are mainly residents of Montana although they travel from great distances within the State. The species taken in order of abundance were rainbow, brook, and cutthroat trout, and Rocky Mountain whitefish. A 5-mile reach of Beaver Creek, which is tributary to this section of the North Fork Sun River, was included in this area.

For type and period of coverage, period of estimates, and expenditures

18

for equipment and annual items, see Gibson Reservoir.

Other expenditure items: See Split Rock Lakes.

Lower Section, North Fork Sun River, Montana (17). The Lower Section
extends downstream from Diversion Reservoir for 22 miles to the confluence of the
North and South Forks Sun River. It is fairly accessible. The average width of
this reach of stream is about 120 feet, and the gradient is moderately steep.
Rainbow trout and Rocky Mountain whitefish appeared most frequently in the catch;
brook and cutthroat trout and suckers also were taken.

Type and period of coverage: Intensive checks on two portions of area
and limited checks on one portion, May 20 through September 30, 1951.

For period of estimates and expenditures for equipment and annual
items, see Gibson Reservoir.

Other expenditure items: See Split Rock Lakes.

Pishkun Canal, Montana (17), which carries water from Diversion Reservoir on the Sun River Irrigation Project to Pishkun Reservoir is 12 miles long
and has a capacity of 1,200 second-feet. Fish enter the canal, and anglers make
moderate use of its waters. Access is good in dry weather by means of a canal
road. Rainbow, cutthroat, and brook trout comprised the most of the catch.

For type and period of coverage, period of estimates, expenditures for
equipment and annual items, and other expenditure items, see Split Rock Lakes.

North Platte River, Wyoming (15), was studied on a highly utilized 5.5-
mile reach of the stream which is in south-central Wyoming on the eastern slope
of the Rocky Mountains. The stream has a good interspersion of pools and riffles
and many side channels, and the water is cold and clear. Access to the river is
good. Fishermen travel from considerable distances to use this area and many

19

nonresident fishermen, especially from Colorado, were attracted to the river.
Rainbow and brown trout comprised most of the catch. Many suckers were taken but
not creeled.

Type and period of coverage: Periodic checks (19), May 1 through
October 15, 1951.

Period of estimates; Fishing season, May 1 through October 15.

Expenditures for equipment and annual items: Applied from a special
survey of Montana fishermen (7).

Other expenditure items: Weighted average, from figures for boat and
shore fishermen.

Lower Section, Madison River, Montana (18). The Madison River is in
the mountains of southwestern Montana. It flows northerly from Yellowstone National Park. Flows are largely controlled by the operation of two onstream
reservoirs. Normally, flows are about 2,000 second-feet during the summer.
The Lower Section extends from Madison Reservoir to Three Forks, Montana, a
distance of 33 miles. Except for an 11-mile reach, this section is characterized by an absence of riffles. Access is fair. In this section of stream
94 percent of the use was by residents, most of whom came from within 50 miles.
Rainbow and brown trout comprised 84 percent of the catch; brook trout, cutthroat
trout, grayling, Rocky Mountain whitefish, and suckers were taken.

Type and period of coverage: Intensive checks, May 21 through September 30, 1950, except in extreme lower portion which was subject to a few patrols.
Limited checks in fall.

Period of estimates: Fishing season, May 21 through October 14, 1950.

For expenditures for equipment and annual items, and other expenditure items, see Madison Reservoir.

Middle Section, Madison River, Montana (18). The Middle Section of 34 miles is between Madison Reservoir and a point about midway between Madison Reservoir and Hebgen Lake. The bed of the river in this section is composed largely or rubble and boulders, and the river is characterized by alternate riffles and pools. The area is generally accessible. Of the use in this reach of stream, 22 percent was by nonresidents. Rainbow and brown trout and Rocky Mountain whitefish comprised most of the catch. Other fishes taken included suckers, grayling, and brook and cutthroat trout.

Type and period of coverage: Intensive checks, May 20 through September 30, 1951. Limited checks of lower portion in fall.

Period of estimates: Fishing season, June 16 through November 15 on lower portion, May 20 through September 30 on upper portion.

Expenditure for equipment and annual items: See Madison Reservoir.

Other expenditure items: One basic expenditure figure derived.

Upper Section, Madison River, Montana (18). This 31-mile section extends from the Middle Section to Hebgen Dam and is somewhat similar to the Middle Section, although the gradient is a little steeper and there are more rapids. Access is excellent. Fifty-five percent of the use was by nonresidents, probably because of the natural attractiveness of the area and proximity to Yellowstone National Park. Utah chubs were taken in this area in addition to species listed for the Middle Section.

Type and period of coverage: Intensive checks, May 18 through September 30, 1952.

Period of estimates: Fishing season, same as above period.

For expenditures for equipment and annual items, and other expenditure items, see Hebgen Reservoir.

21

PRINCIPAL CREEL-CENSUS and EXPENDITURE DATA

Fisherman use in terms of total fisherman days and fisherman days per
surface acre of reservoir (or lake) or per mile of stream, yield in terms of numbers and pounds of fish per hour, total number and poundage of fish, and pounds
of fish per surface acre or per mile of stream, and expenditures per person per
day, total for area, per pound of fish, and per surface acre or per mile of
stream, are shown for 26 areas studied in the Missouri River Basin between 1947
and 1952 in tables 1, 2, 3, and 4.

Creel census data demonstrate tremendous variations in use and yield
of the many situations studied. These data for those areas studied more than
one year also demonstrate that there can be considerable variation in use and
yield from one year to the next on a particular area. A few of the more obvious
factors contributing to these variations, such as ease of access, nearness to
centers of population, and natural attractiveness of an area, are indicated in the
description of the areas, but it is impossible to make any generalization of
correlation.

Examination of data shown in the accompanying tables indicates that
fisherman expenditures per day are generally higher for cold-water fishermen
than for warm-water fishermen. On the average, cold-water fishermen spend
roughly twice as much per day as warm-water fishermen. Two factors seem im-
portant: (1) Cold-water fishermen spend more for equipment, and (2) cold-water
fishermen are inclined to travel greater distances to fish and thus not only
have larger transportation expenses but also have more trip expenses. Other
expenditure figures shown in the tables, of course, are dependent upon the use
and yield of the particular fishery and thus vary accordingly.

22

A - WARM-WATER RE...OIRS AND LAKES

Name	State	Year									
Ocean Lake (1,2)	Wyoming	1947 (Summer)	6,100	7,639 }8,433	1.3 }1.4	8.30	2.98	206,600 }220,800	74,100 }81,800	12.13 }13.4	$ 9.26
		1947 (Winter)		794	0.3	8.70	4.72	14,200	7,700	1.3	71.58
		1948 (Summer)	6,100	15,711 }16,255	2.6 }2.7	5.20	1.94	253,600 }260,500	94,800 }97,400	15.55 }15.9	9.02
		1948 (Winter)		441	0.1	5.70	2.15	6,900	2,600	0.4	11.58
Lake Maloney (3,4)	Nebraska	1948	1,670	18,000	10.8	0.88	0.70	50,000	40,000	24.0	2.42
		1949	1,670	15,259	9.1	0.24	0.32	18,700	24,660	14.8	2.42
Fort Peck Reservoir (9)	Montana	1948	245,000	151,450	0.1	0.66	0.30	16,000	23,630	0.10	3.13
		1949	245,000	16,300	0.1	0.78	0.35	48,910	22,150	0.09	3.06
		1950	245,000	20,380	0.1	0.58	0.44	53,800	40,700	0.17	2.75
Split Rock Lakes (17)	Montana	1951	120	516	4.3	0.06	0.23		201	6.2	5.91
Angostura Reservoir (11)	South Dakota	1952	5,600	41,018	7.3	1.25	0.50	223,668	89,843	6.2	5.91
Cottonwood Lake (12)	South Dakota	1952	1,450	16,495	11.4	1.65	0.76	96,472	44,182	16.0	4.80
Harry Strunk Lake (16)	Nebraska	1952	1,768	55,000	31.1	0.51	0.40	131,000	103,000	30.5	2.79
										58.3	3.16
Missouri River (9)	Montana	1948	12	2,600	800.0	0.75	0.77	22,100	22,600	1,883.3	$ 3.13
		1949	12	5,750	479.2	0.70	0.67	12,520	11,940	995.0	3.06
		1950	12	5,790	482.5	0.48	0.45	7,180	6,960	580.0	2.75
Republican River (8)	Nebraska and Kansas	1951	43	17,426	405.3	0.09	0.18	6,538	13,021	302.6	1.80
Medicine Creek (16)	Nebraska	1951	1-3/4	1/5,000	—	—	—	1/15,000	1/20,000	11,428.6	3.16
				2,857.1							

ck Reservoir and Harry Strunk Lake are not comparable to the Republican River fishery; therefore, this figure has no real meaning.

TABLE 3. CREEL-CENSUS AND EXPENDITURE DATA - COLD-WATER RESERVOIRS AND LAKES

Fishery	State	Year	Surface acres	Utilization		Fish per hour of effort	Pounds of fish per hour of effort	Yield			Expenditure			
				Total fisherman days	Fisherman days per acre			Total No. fish	Total poundage of fish	Pounds per surface acre	Per person per day	Total on area	Per surface acre	Per pound of fish
Deerfield Reservoir (5,14)	South Dakota	1949	435	6,720	15.4	0.42	0.25	19,380	11,680	26.9	$5.20	$34,944.00	$2.99	$80.33
		1950	435	8,190	18.8	0.48	0.20	23,400	9,620	22.1	5.20	42,594.00	4.43	97.90
Pathfinder Reservoir (10)	Wyoming	1951	22,600	7,850	0.3	0.15	0.31	7,050	14,400	0.6	7.22	56,677.00	3.94	2.51
Alcova Reservoir (10)	Wyoming	1951	2,500	4,750	1.9	0.26	0.22	6,050	5,100	2.0	5.79	27,502.50	5.39	11.00
Gibson Reservoir (17)	Montana	1951	1,360	895	0.7	4.8	0.29	1,903	1,415	1.0	6.57	5,880.15	4.16	4.32
Diversion Reservoir (17)	Montana	1951	100	2,328	23.3	0.33	0.14	4,321	1,878	18.8	5.01	11,709.48	7.33	137.58
Willow Creek Reservoir (17)	Montana	1951	1,400	202	0.1	0.18	0.25	191	270	0.2	5.91	1,193.82	4.42	0.85
Fishbun Reservoir (17)	Montana	1951	1,550	1,575	1.0	0.07	0.10	534	759	0.5	5.91	9,308.25	12.26	6.01
Tunnel Lake (17)	Montana	1951	30	504	16.8	0.11	0.12	359	299	10.0	5.91	2,978.64	9.96	99.29
Wood Lake( ) (17)	Montana	1951	50	305	19.3	0.26	0.11	494	197	10.0	6.14	2,363.90	11.88	119.20
Madison Reservoir (18)	Montana	1950	3,900	7,972	2.1	0.32	0.39	14,797	18,144	4.8	7.90	62,978.80	3.47	16.57
Hebgen Lake (18)	Montana	1952	13,400	10,440	0.8	0.30	0.37	13,258	16,153	1.2	13.08	132,631.20	8.21	9.90
Weighted Average - Expenditures											$7.63		$4.92	$8.25

1/ For 2-week period only, but probably represents most of the fishing.

TABLE 4. CREEL-CENSUS AND EXPENDITURE DATA - COLD-WATER STREAMS

Fishery	State	Year	Miles of stream	Utilization		Fish per hour of effort	Pounds of fish per hour of effort	Yield			Expenditure			
				Total fisherman days	Fisherman days per mile of stream			Total No. fish	Total poundage of fish	Pounds per mile of stream	Per person per day	Total on area	Per pound of fish	Per mile of stream
West Gallatin River, Middle Section (6,13)	Montana	1949	28	11,100	396.4	0.57	0.36	16,100	10,300	367.9	$4.48	$49,728.00	$4.83	$1,776.00
		1950	28	13,100	467.4	0.51	0.35	16,300	10,900	691.8	4.48	59,696.00	5.19	2,066.00
West Gallatin River, Upper Section (6,13)1/	Montana	1949	55	15,00	272.7	1.07	0.41	39,900	15,000	272.7	4.48	67,200.00	1.68	1,221.42
Fork of Gallatin (North Platte River) (10)	Wyoming	1951	4	1,350	337.5	0.21	0.21	1,050	1,900	475.0	6.48	8,761.50	4.61	2,190.38
North Fork Sun River, Upper Section (17)	Montana	1951	50	668	13.4	0.31	0.23	1,129	832	16.6	10.70	7,147.60	8.59	142.95
North Fork Sun River, Middle Section (17)	Montana	1951	8	2,020	252.5	0.47	0.13	3,707	1,073	134.1	5.91	11,938.20	11.13	1,492.28
North Fork Sun River, Lower Section (17)	Montana	1951	22	1,290	58.6	0.72	0.30	3,595	1,510	68.6	5.91	7,623.90	5.05	346.54
Fishbun Canal (17)	Montana	1951	12	179	14.9	0.56	0.19	260	87	7.3	5.91	1,057.89	12.16	88.16
Madison River, Lower Section (18)	Montana	1950	33	8,107	245.7	0.43	0.44	18,798	19,352	586.4	7.90	64,045.30	3.31	1,940.77
Madison River, Middle Section (18)	Montana	1951	34	7,307	214.9	0.62	0.54	19,291	17,139	504.1	7.95	58,090.65	3.39	1,708.55
Madison River, Upper Section (18)	Montana	1951	3	7,246	233.1	0.55	0.47	14,335	11,894	393.1	13.08	94,777.76	7.97	3,057.34
North Platte River (15)	Wyoming	1951	5-1/2	6,847	1,244.9	0.57	0.40	15,293	10,603	1,927.8	15.45	105,786.15	9.98	19,233.84
Weighted Average - Expenditures											$5.44			$1,530.11

1/ Not included in weighted average since expenditures were arbitrarily estimated from data secured on the Middle Section, West Gallatin River.

LIST OF REFERENCES

Reference
No.

1. Fish and Wildlife Service

   1950a. An evaluation of the Ocean Lake Fishery, Wyoming, 1947-1949.
   U. S. Fish and Wild. Ser., Mo. Riv. Basin Studies, 15 pp.
   (Mimeo.)

2. 1950b. A two-year creel census, Ocean Lake, Wyoming, U. S. Fish and
   Wild. Ser., Mo. Riv. Basin Studies, 18 pp. (Mimeo.)

3. 1950c. An evaluation of the Lake Maloney, Nebraska, fishery. U. S.
   Fish and Wild. Ser., Mo. Riv. Basin Studies, 10 pp. (Mimeo.)

4. 1951a. A two-year creel census of Lake Maloney, Nebraska, 1948-1949.
   U. S. Fish and Wild. Ser., Mo. Riv. Basin Studies, 23 pp.
   (Mimeo.)

5. 1951b. A two-year creel census, Deerfield Reservoir, South Dakota,
   1949-1950. U. S. Fish and Wild. Ser., Mo. Riv. Basin
   Studies, 26 pp. (Mimeo.)

6. 1951c. A two-year fishery investigation, West Gallatin River, Montana,
   1949-1950. U. S. Fish and Wild. Ser., Mo. Riv. Basin Studies,
   42 pp. (Mimeo.)

7. 1951d. Annual and investment expenditures of Montana sportsmen, 1949.
   U. S. Fish and Wild. Ser., Mo. Riv. Basin Studies, 35 pp.
   (Mimeo.)

8. 1952a. A one-year creel census and evaluation of the Republican River,
   Nebraska & Kansas, 1951. U. S. Fish and Wild. Ser., Mo. Riv.
   Basin Studies, 29 pp. (Mimeo.)

9. 1952b. A three-year fishery investigation, Fort Peck Reservoir,
   Montana, 1948-1950. U. S. Fish and Wild. Ser., Mo. Riv. Basin
   Studies, 49 pp. (Mimeo.)

10. 1952c. One-year creel census and fisherman expenditure study, Alcova
    and Pathfinder Reservoirs, North Platte River, Wyoming. U. S.
    Fish and Wild. Ser., Mo. Riv. Basin Studies, 43 pp. (Mimeo.)

11. 1953a. Creel census and fisherman expenditure study, Angostura Reser-
    voir, South Dakota, 1952. U. S. Fish and Wild. Ser., Mo. Riv.
    Basin Studies, 17 pp. (Mimeo.)

27

12. Fish and Wildlife Service (continued)

1953b. Creel census and fisherman-expenditure study, Cottonwood Lake, South Dakota, 1952. U. S. Fish and Wild. Ser., Mo. Riv. Basin Studies, 18 pp. (Mimeo.)

13. 1953c. Fisherman-expenditure study, West Gallatin River, Montana, 1949-1950. U. S. Fish and Wild. Ser., Mo. Riv. Basin Studies, 11 pp. (Mimeo.)

14. 1953d. Fisherman-expenditure study, Deerfield Reservoir, South Dakota, 1949-1950. U. S. Fish and Wild. Ser., Mo. Riv. Basin Studies, 10 pp. (Mimeo.)

15. 1953e. Fishery investigation, North Platte River, Wyoming, 1952. U. S. Fish and Wild. Ser., Mo. Riv. Basin Studies, 16 pp. (Mimeo.)

16. 1953f. Fishery investigation, Harry Strunk Lake, Nebraska, 1952. U. S. Fish and Wild. Ser., Mo. Riv. Basin Studies, 23 pp. (Mimeo.)

17. 1954a. Creel census and expenditure study, North Fork Sun River, Montana, 1951. U. S. Fish and Wild. Ser., Spec. Sci. Rept.: Fish. No. 120, 39 pp.

18. 1954b. Creel census and expenditure study, Madison River, Montana, 1950-1952. U. S. Fish and Wild. Ser., Spec. Sci. Rept.: Fish. No. 126, 39 pp.

19. Jeppson, Paul W.

1951. Analysis of basin-wide creel census technique. U. S. Fish and Wild. Ser., Mo. Riv. Basin Studies, 7 pp. (Mimeo.) (Statement presented at mid-winter conference of all Missouri River Basin Studies personnel, Billings, Montana, January 29 to February 2, 1951.)

28

CPSIA information can be obtained
at www.ICGtesting.com
Printed in the USA
LVHW081107301118
598533LV00049B/1218/P